Powerful Ideas
Establishing National Parks

Written by Mary-Anne Creasy
Series Consultant: Linda Hoyt

T0359787

WorldWise
Content-based Learning

Contents

Introduction

Around the world there are some areas that are so amazing that it is decided that their natural environment must be preserved. They are national parks and they must be protected. A national park may have historical or scientific interest, or be set aside for public recreation and enjoyment. It is important to **preserve** these areas, their accompanying plant and animal life, and the cultural link with people who lived there in the past.

Not ours –
but ours to look after

The authorities and **rangers** who manage national parks educate visitors to take care of the environment and wildlife. There are strict regulations about what people can and cannot do in the parks. Usually people are not allowed to leave rubbish behind or make contact with animals. Some parks allow visitors to travel only in limited areas to protect the environment and wildlife.

Chapter 1

Some of the earliest national parks

The United States is well known around the world as one of the first countries to establish a national park, but did you know that the world's oldest national park is in Mongolia?

Find out more

How many national parks are there in Mongolia today?

Bogd Khan Uul National Park, Mongolia

In 1778, the Mongolian governor appealed to the emperor to **preserve** the natural beauty and spiritual significance of Bogd Khan Uul. It was the first protected wilderness area, or national park, in the world. The mountain in this area is over 2,000 metres high and is surrounded by coniferous forest trees, steppe grasslands, alpine **tundra** and rocky desert.

It has over 200 species of plants, rare animals, such as Siberian deer, wild boar, musk deer, and many species of birds, such as the common buzzard and woodpecker.

In 1996, UNESCO listed Bogd Khan Uul as a World Heritage Biosphere Reserve.

Fact file
Established: 1778
Size: About 67,000 hectares
Location: Southern Mongolia in Khentii Mountains area
Managed by: Mongolian Government

Yellowstone National Park, United States

In 1871, the US government surveyed a region of northwest Wyoming. This area's great natural beauty was painted and photographed. Its geysers, hot springs, waterfalls, lakes, forests and alpine meadows were considered significant. In 1872, the US government passed a law declaring the region of Yellowstone a national park, the first in the USA. Over the years, more wilderness area surrounding the original park has been set aside, and today it is considered a unique **ecosystem**.

Fact file

Established: 1872
Size: About 900,000 hectares
Location: Northwest region of United States in Wyoming, Montana and Idaho
Managed by:
US National Park Service

Yellowstone National Park is a single, vast tract of land that teaches us how nature works.

Each year, millions of people visit Yellowstone to see its natural wonders. They camp, hike, take photographs and marvel at the many and varied plants and animals that live there.

Find out more

How did Old Faithful geyser get its name?

Yellowstone contains almost half of the world's geysers. The most famous geyser is Old Faithful.

9

Royal National Park, Australia

Australia's first national park, Royal National Park, features sandstone cliffs, gorges, waterfalls and native **vegetation**. It is located south of Sydney, the capital city of New South Wales. Conservationists lobbied the government of the time to protect the land and its wildlife from farmers and introduced European animals. It became a national park in 1879. The park joins with the Blue Mountains National Park, Morton National Park and surrounding protected nature reserves.

Fact file

Established: 1879
Size: Over 15,000 hectares
Location: South of Sydney, New South Wales
Managed by: NSW National Parks and Wildlife Service in collaboration with the local Dharawal people

Did you know?

A nature reserve is a protected area that has high conservation value.

One of Australia's newest national parks, the nearby
Dharawal National Park, was declared in 2012 to protect
several ancient Aboriginal sites. **Rangers** take students
and tourists on guided walks to teach them about
Aboriginal knowledge of and interaction with the local
environment. They identify the park's natural features as
well as the ancient **shell middens**, **sacred** places and rock
engravings that are found in the area.

Tongariro National Park, New Zealand

The original size of New Zealand's first national park, Tongariro, was around 3,000 hectares. Over the past century it has increased to almost 80,000 hectares. The park has three active volcanoes – Tongariro, Ngauruhoe and Ruapehu – as well as emerald lakes and boiling mud pools. It is home to the famous Tongariro Alpine Crossing and other beautiful hiking tracks and ski fields.

In 1990, Tongariro National Park was declared a **World Heritage Site** in recognition of its outstanding natural characteristics.

Fact file

Established: 1887
Size: Almost 80,000 hectares
Location: North Island, New Zealand
Managed by: Department of Conservation Te Papa Atawhai

A Maōri legend

The Tongariro region is of great significance to Maōri people, and there are many legends from the area. According to one legend, the high priest Ngatoroirangi, who was prominent during the settling and exploration of Aotearoa (New Zealand), was saved from being frozen to death in a snowstorm while exploring Mount Tongariro. Near death, he called to his two sisters to send him the sacred fire that they had brought with them from Hawaiki, the traditional home of the Maōri people. The fire arrived just in time to save him from freezing to death.

Banff National Park, Canada

Banff is Canada's oldest national park and was established in 1885. It is located in the Rocky Mountains, west of Calgary in the Province of Alberta.

Mountainous terrain, numerous **glaciers** and ice fields, dense coniferous forest and alpine landscapes ensure that this is one of the world's most beautiful and well-known regions.

The establishment of Banff National Park was **contentious**. Some groups wanted to commercialise the hot springs in the area, while others wanted to protect the place. Today, there are strict rules about new developments. It is considered more important to conserve than harm the wilderness.

Fact file

Established: 1885
Size: 664,100 hectares
Location: West of Calgary, Alberta
Managed by: Parks Canada

When the park was first established, the **indigenous** people were excluded from traditional hunting and gathering, and there was little information about their ancestors who lived there. Over the past 50 years however, this has changed and today nearly 90 per cent of Canada's national parks are managed in accordance with treaties or agreements with indigenous peoples.

The Buffalo Nations Luxton Museum in Banff is dedicated to the First Nations of North America.

Chapter 2

A man of powerful ideas

John Muir

John Muir

Many national parks have been established as the result of activities of passionate individuals raising public awareness of particular natural places. The most instrumental and famous advocate for lobbying the protection and conservation of wilderness areas was John Muir.

A man of nature

John Muir emigrated, with his family, from Scotland to the United States in 1849 when he was just 11 years old.

They settled in Wisconsin in the Midwest. This new landscape of open spaces, mountains and plant life stirred Muir's interest in plants and **geology**. He learned to love the outdoors and, as a young man, he studied **botany**, geology and chemistry.

Fox River in Burlington, Wisconsin, USA

Through his studies, he came to realise that to truly learn about nature, he had to be surrounded by it, and so Muir started hiking through the North American wilderness.

His first major hike was in 1864, when he made his way to Canada. Later, he wrote about his experience in an article. It was his first article in a magazine and it revealed Muir's passion for nature. He admitted that he had more joy from seeing the beautiful flowers than he did from meeting most humans.

In 1868, Muir went to live in the wilderness of Yosemite. He built a cabin in the woods and for the next two years he lived, worked and explored the Yosemite area. He took notes about the landforms, plants, rainfall, clouds and temperature, and these observations later became a guidebook to the area.

Muir's knowledge and careful observation of plant life led him to discover rare orchid species.

New discoveries

Although John Muir had never formally completed his university studies, his knowledge of geology was sound, and his observations at Yosemite were thorough and convincing. In 1871, he challenged the scientific community's belief that the deep valleys in the landscape around Yosemite had been formed by earthquakes, and suggested instead that **glaciers** had carved these stunning valleys. Scientists became interested in this theory and he was encouraged to make further studies.

In 1872, Muir criticised the Californian government for neglecting Yosemite Valley and for allowing people to claim the land for farming and logging. He believed the valley should be completely off-limits to farmers, loggers and anyone else who could disturb or harm the place.

Over the next 17 years, Muir travelled extensively, studying and researching wilderness areas. He gave lectures and wrote articles about the wilderness that he observed. These articles captured the imagination of people and his career as a writer and environmental **activist** took off.

President Theodore Roosevelt with John Muir on a camping trip to Yosemite

A president goes camping

In 1903, Muir convinced President Theodore Roosevelt to go camping with him in Yosemite Valley. His aim was to persuade the president to expand the boundaries of the park. The president was impressed with the beauty of the area and agreed. Just three years later, in 1906, Yosemite National Park was expanded to include Yosemite Valley and Mariposa Grove.

? Did you know?

Although Yosemite Valley represents only one per cent of the national park, it is the main attraction in the park and is where most visitors arrive and stay.

President Theodore Roosevelt (fourth from left) in front of a massive, ancient giant sequoia

19

Chapter 3

The Sierra Club

Protecting national parks

Through John Muir's environmental work and his experience of establishing Yosemite as a national park, he knew there were many more wilderness areas that needed to be saved from environmental damage. He also knew that farmers, timber companies, mining companies and others would continue to lobby the government to allow them to exploit Yosemite and other protected areas.

So in 1892, he helped create the Sierra Club, an organisation that set out to protect national parks, and took action to **preserve** large tracts of land. Muir was elected the Sierra Club's first president.

Muir's influence

The Sierra Club became very influential and attracted many members. It published a magazine called *Sierra*, for which Muir wrote many articles. In one, he encouraged the public to observe and enjoy the wilderness of Yellowstone National Park and wrote:

Of the four national parks of the West, the Yellowstone is far the largest. It is a big, wholesome wilderness on the broad summit of the Rocky Mountains ... the park is full of exciting wonders .... The wildest geysers in the world ... it is a hard place to leave, you will remember these fine, wild views, and look back with joy to your wanderings in the blessed old Yellowstone Wonderland.

Visiting Australia

In 1903, John Muir visited Australia. The Sierra Club magazine recorded some details of this visit:

John Muir visited Australia as part of his 1903–1904 world tour. John Muir visited zoological and botanical gardens and parks in Fremantle, Melbourne and Sydney. He travelled inland to see the eucalytus forests of the Great Dividing Range and took the train from Sydney to Mt Victoria in the Blue Mountains to see the Jenolan Caves. He went to Queensland to see the Hoop Pine and saw the Great Barrier Reef from his ship.

A eucalyptus forest

Melbourne Botanic Gardens

Contributing to wilderness conservation

1893 US President Benjamin Harrison establishes the Sierra Forest Reserve after petitions were sent from the Sierra Club to the government

1898 The Sierra Club helps to establish parks to preserve coastal redwoods in California

1899 Mt Rainier National Park is established after the Sierra Club and several other organisations lobby the US government to protect the area

1916 The Sierra Club supports and helps to establish the National Park Service

1920 The Sierra Club succeeds in opposing a plan to build dams in Yellowstone National Park

1964 After years of battle, the US government passes the Wilderness Act, the first wilderness protection legislation in the world

2012 Influenced by club petitions, the US Department of the Interior releases a plan to protect four million hectares of the Western Arctic Reserve from oil and gas drilling

The Sierra Club today

Today, the Sierra Club continues its work to expand areas of wilderness protection. It is now the most influential grassroots environmental organisation in the United States and has over three million members and supporters.

The Sierra Club has also extended its work beyond wilderness conservation. It has recently been active in influencing the US government to close 251 coal-fired power stations with its **campaign** to achieve a clean energy future. It works with partners across the world to build awareness about **fossil fuels**, working towards a safe, sustainable future with access to clean energy for all.

Glacier Bay National Park, Alaska

The Sierra Club, America's most influential environmental organisation, works to protect national parks in the United States.

Arches National Park, Utah

Chapter 4

Father and son activists

Myles Dunphy

The Australian wilderness movement began in the early years of the 20th century. A key figure of the movement was Myles Dunphy, a man who had a passion for the environment and love of the outdoors.

Born in 1891, Dunphy, like John Muir, had early childhood bushwalking experiences that were a source of inspiration to protect the wilderness. In 1910, as an architecture student, Dunphy spent a week bushwalking with friends at Katoomba. This began a lifelong love for the Blue Mountains and it was where he started his conservation work.

In 1914, he assisted in the formation of the Mountain Trails Club of New South Wales. While on extended walks and camping trips, he sketched and compiled a series of detailed maps for newly developed walking trails within the Blue Mountains area near Sydney.

Myles Dunphy (left), with friends on a camping trip in the Blue Mountains

A map created by Myles Dunphy of an area in the Blue Mountains

For six decades, from 1916 through to the 1970s, Dunphy was involved in many **campaigns** to protect bushland from development. His conservation work contributed to the establishment of a number of national parks and wilderness areas.

Dunphy was a foundation member of the Sydney Bushwalkers' Club in 1927. He and the club helped save the Blue Gum Forest on the Grose River in New South Wales from being logged.

Dunphy knew how much John Muir and the Sierra Club had achieved in establishing national parks in the United States and, over the years, he publicised a number of proposals to encourage protected environments in New South Wales. In 1959, his dream was achieved and the Greater Blue Mountains National Park was established.

During his lifetime, Myles Dunphy received recognition for the important work he did for conservation in New South Wales.

"Whether we like it or not, we hold our land in trust for our successors." – Myles Dunphy

In his father's footsteps: Milo Dunphy

Milo Dunphy, like his father, also became a renowned **environmentalist** with an exuberant passion for forests. Born in 1929, he was part of almost all environmental campaigns across Australia in the last half of the 20th century.

In 1972, he became the founding director of the Total Environment Centre, which acted to set aside areas of national park.

Like John Muir, Milo worked at a political level and took politicians and people of influence into the bush where he shared his enthusiasm for the wilderness and showed them how important it was to protect such places. He was most successful in influencing state laws in New South Wales to expand the state's national parks area from two per cent to almost five per cent. In 1986, he was awarded an Order of Australia for his services to conservation.

Wilderness area preserved in Australian Parliament House

The Shoalhaven River runs through cliffs and tall, dense eucalypt forests in southern New South Wales until it forms an estuary on the Pacific Ocean near Nowra. The famous Australian artist, Arthur Boyd, painted the landscape around the Shoalhaven River to show the uniqueness of the Australian landscape. In the 1980s, a tapestry based on one of Boyd's paintings of the Shoalhaven was commissioned for Parliament House. The tapestry took over two years to complete and covers most of the back wall of the Great Hall, known as the "room of the land". The artwork conveys the beauty, wildness and vastness of the Australian landscape and captures visitors' full attention.

Find out more

Milo Dunphy was involved in trying to save Lake Pedder in Tasmania from being dammed. Find out more about what happened at Lake Pedder in the 1960s and 70s.

The Dunphy legacy

The Dunphy family's conservation work continues through the Dunphy Wilderness Fund which, since 1996, has donated one million dollars each year for the purchase of wilderness land.

The Total Environment Centre honours Myles and Milo Dunphy in its continued activity to create new national parks across Australia. It works to protect green spaces, water catchments, forests and their wildlife, and to reduce pollution.

The centre generates community-focused campaigns, encourages citizen science and publishes reports making recommendations to government on saving bushland and biodiversity. Its campaigns include the *SOS Green Spaces* and *Living Landscapes* projects. The first of these is an interactive map to which people can add a patch of endangered green space or bushland, and the other appeals to people to take action to reset the balance between humans, plants and animals, and create strong laws that protect the environment.

Find out more

Find out more about the Total Environment Centre and how you can help protect the environment.

Conclusion

Individuals can make a difference. Their ideas can help bring about change if they can inspire others to help them. They can write persuasive, passionate articles and books. They can use scientific observations and evidence to win over doubters. Most importantly, passionate **environmentalists** like John Muir in the United States, and Myles and Milo Dunphy in Australia showed us that their powerful ideas and personalities influenced people to change laws and protect the environment.

These conservationists persuaded their politicians that the preservation of their country's pristine natural environment was as important as the protection of the great monuments and buildings of Europe. Their powerful ideas are now translated into a whole system of national parks on the west coast of the United States and throughout Australia.

As well as fostering powerful ideas, they were inspirational in influencing other powerful people and made deep, lasting impressions on those who met them.

What you can do

Visit a nearby national park or nature reserve.

Talk to a park ranger to learn about how to protect national parks.

Join a conservation group with your friends and family. Volunteer to remove rubbish and weeds from a local park or bushland area.

Attend a community tree planting day with your family.

Glossary

activist a person who supports a belief or cause that he or she feels strongly about

botany the scientific study of plants

campaign a series of ongoing events aimed at achieving a particular result

contentious something that is likely to cause disagreement

ecosystem a whole system of living things that depend on each other for survival

environmentalist a person who works to protect the natural environment

fossil fuels fuels such as oil, gas or coal which are made from the remains of ancient plant and animal fossils in the earth

geology the science of the history of Earth, especially through the study of rocks

glaciers slow-moving rivers of ice that form when snow is compacted

indigenous the first people to live in a country or area

preserve to stop places or things from being harmed or destroyed

rangers keepers of parks, forests or parts of the countryside

sacred extremely precious

shell midden a mound containing shells, animal bones or other discarded items that indicates the site of a human settlement

tundra flat, treeless, very cold areas of land found in the Arctic region

UNESCO United Nations Educational, Scientific, and Cultural Organization

vegetation the plants that cover an area of land

World Heritage Site a place of world significance

Index